Virtual Reality in Music Production and Composition

Creating Melodies for a New Era

Table of Contents

Chapter 1. Introduction

Immerse yourself into a symphony of innovation and creativity with our Special Report entitled, "Virtual Reality in Music Production and Composition: Creating Melodies for a New Era". This enlightening exploration ventures into the cutting-edge intersections of technology, artistry, and sound. Don't worry, we propel you through this radical journey with an easy-to-grasp, down-to-earth approach, unveiling how virtual reality is revolutionizing both the process of creating music and the very essence of melodic arrangement. Whether you're a seasoned producer, an aspiring composer, or a music enthusiast, this watershed report offers a memorable tour, demystifying the technical jargon to reveal the harmony of innovation. This leap into the future of music might just strike a chord with you, enticing you to tune into the overwhelming potential of the fusion of music and VR. Ready to conduct your curiosity into this new era of musical composition? Read on!

Chapter 2. The Harmony of Innovation: A Prelude to VR in Music

In the realm of music, boundaries are perceived as challenges and innovation is the tool wielded to overcome them. As digital technology progresses, artists now discover themselves with a wealth of new tools to explore expanding horizons of creativity. Among these instruments lies the potential of Virtual Reality (VR), the combination of audio, visual, and often haptic input to create deeply immersive experiences.

2.1. The Promise of VR in Music

Ever since its inception, VR has consistently stepped out of its conventional use in gaming and simulations to show incredible promise across an array of creative disciplines. In the realm of music, specifically, VR introduces a radical shift in how composers and producers approach their craft. It allows them to visualize music in a three-dimensional space, creating an intuitive, multisensory method to interact with sound. This interplay between music composition and advanced technology is, as modern composer Björk beautifully phrases it, "a new stage for our ballet with technology and sound, a more multi-sensory, more immersive approach."

One might imagine standing inside their sound canvas, able to manipulate spatial soundscapes with a wave of their hand or even create music with their movements. Others may envision the capacity to host and attend immersive live concerts in a virtual space, tapping the boundless design potential of a VR environment. These realities are not far fetched but are testament to the possibilities VR brings to music creation and enjoyment.

2.2. The VR Music Creation Process

A significant role of VR in music composition is the evolution of the music creation process. Traditional music production software (Digital Audio Workstations or DAWs) offers a two-dimensional approach to arranging sound-- layers of sound represented as lines stacked on top of each other. With the introduction of VR, artists can conceptualize and interact with the melodies, harmonies, and rhythms around them in a three-dimensional soundscape.

VR music creation tools like SoundStage VR, AliveIn Tech's Tranzient, or Virtuoso, allow producers to play, program, and record music by interacting with virtual musical instruments and equipment in a simulated studio. A melody can be sculpted, a bass line drawn and beats "painted" into the VR space. This technology opens up a new pathway for conventional music creators to visualize sound in a remarkable manner that wasn't possible before.

2.3. Sonic Spatialization and Immersion

Aside from reshaping the music creation process, VR also influences music on the listening end. With VR, listeners can experience music in a more immersive, spatial, and interactive way. Spatial audio, or 360-degree sound, is critical for immersive VR experiences. It lets the sound move around the listener and even allows them to interact with individual sounds within the song. Virtual concerts, like the immersive musical experience provided by TheWaveVR, provide listeners with an engaging, multi-sensory concert experience.

Exploiting the immersive potential of VR also opens up new possibilities for music therapy. Research has suggested that music, when paired with VR, can have a profound impact on rehabilitation for patients with various neurological conditions. By placing patients in a controlled and motivating virtual environment, music-based VR therapies have shown promising results in improving motor functions and cognitive processing speed.

2.4. The VR Evolution: Challenges and Opportunities

While VR holds a promise for the future of music, it is important to recognize its current limitations and the challenges it must overcome. These include technical barriers like latency and motion sickness, and the high costs of VR equipment, making it less accessible to everyone. However, these hurdles are not insurmountable, and with continuous advancements in technology and growing interest in the field, it won't be long before they are overcome.

On the upside, the integration of AI and VR will provide composers with a new palette of intelligent tools to generate music and create immersive experiences. Companies like Google Magenta are already experimenting with AI, enabling artists to create music leveraging AI-powered VR platforms.

2.5. Final Note: The VR Symphony of the Future

As we stand today, the intersection of VR and music remains a nascent, untread path of innovation, begging to be explored. But the composition is far from complete. The true harmony will emerge when VR becomes an intuitive and integral part of the music creation process and a commonplace in our music consumption.

Artists and technologists are continuously shaping this bold symphony for the future. As the lines between the physical and virtual world continue to blur, we're inching closer to the melody of a new era where VR shapes the way we create, consume, and perceive music.

So, we welcome you to this grand overture—a prelude to the era of VR in music. A harmony of innovation awaits you, ready to strike a chord with the trends of the future.

Chapter 3. From Analog to Digital: VR's Role in Transforming Music Production

The winds of change have been seamlessly transforming the music industry, from humble vinyl records and clunky reel tapes, to the dominant digital formats of the modern era. Galloping progress in technology now nudges us to yet another evolutionary frontier—Virtual Reality (VR).

3.1. The Evolution of Music Production

Music production has always been inextricably entwined with the development of technology. The earliest music recordings, implemented with the help of phonographs in the late 19th century, were skeins of sound wrapped around a cylinder. By the 20th century, technological inventions saw music etching onto vinyl records, shifting later to magnetic tapes. However, the true revolution came with the onset of digital recording, which opened up unlimited possibilities for editing, manipulating, mixing, and sharing music.

The transition from analog to digital utterly redefined the borders of the sonic landscape. The mystique of the recording studio was unveiled as these tools found their way into the hands of the masses. It was no longer exclusive to a privileged set of artists working with recording labels. Today, a teenager with a laptop and the right software can produce music that rivals the quality of a professional studio recording.

Now, imagine if this process were taken a step further. Picture being able to virtually step into the music, manipulate the elements in a 3D space, and interact with sound like never before, thanks to VR.

3.2. Bridging Reality: How VR is Changing Music Creation

The meticulous task of music production—recording, editing, and mixing—traditionally requires expensive studio equipment and a deep knowledge of audio engineering. Virtual Reality in music production can potentially democratize this process further. One can don a pair of VR goggles and be instantly transported to a virtual studio with an array of tools and instruments at their fingertips.

Creating music in VR is akin to painting on a blank canvas within immersive 360 degrees. It breaks down the linear wall between musician and instrument, fostering a more intuitive and interactive process. The dual-hand controllers serve as an extension of the artist themselves, allowing for direct manipulation of the multiple elements in the spatial audio environment.

More than a gadget for playback, VR lets creators step inside their composition, offering unique perspectives to intricacies within the music. Simply put, VR takes a primarily auditory medium and adds a powerful visual element that enhances creativity and interaction.

3.3. Virtual Instruments: Playing with a New Reality

Virtual instruments are not new. Synthesizers and digital audio workstations have provided computer-generated sounds for decades. But virtual reality introduces an entirely different concept—an immersive virtual instrument.

Inside VR, sound design becomes a tactile experience. You could walk around a sound, reach out and alter it, or pick up an instrument that doesn't even exist in reality. VR music creation tools like LyraVR, EXA: The Infinite Instrument, and SoundStage VR have built unique virtual interfaces for creating music. One could virtually pluck strings floating in the air, slap virtual drums, or play an imaginary saxophone, while composing complex symphonies in a fluid, spatial environment.

3.4. Remixing Reality: VR-based Editing and Mixing

Perhaps the most transformative aspect of VR in music production is in the editing and mixing stages. Visualizing sound in a VR environment offers staggering potentials. Wearing a VR headset, sounds can be represented as visual objects in a virtual 3D space. This allows the manipulation of various elements of a track in a way much more tangible compared to traditional mixing consoles. Changes in pitch, volume, timbre, and more can be seen and adjusted right before one's eyes.

VR programs such as AliveIn Technology's VR MIDI, and Stage, create a visual language for sound, converging the auditory experience with the visual, creating an overall phenomenological experience.

3.5. The Future Awaits: Challenging Boundaries and Prospects

Indeed, the journey to embrace VR in music production isn't without challenges. High cost of VR gear, latency issues, and lack of seasoned professionals well-versed in the VR music production are notable barriers to entry. However, as the technology matures and gains wider acceptance, it will inevitably inspire new methods of music-making while providing unprecedented access to music production.

In tandem, the industry needs to cultivate an education ecosystem to build skills and proliferate knowledge about VR music production. User-friendly interfaces, intuitive VR instruments, and cost-effective VR tools will be crucial to making this technology more accessible.

As we witness the transformation from analog to digital to virtual, it becomes clear that we're moving closer to a reality where the creation, recording, and performance of music are fused into an immersive, interactive, tactile experience. This is not only exciting from a technological perspective, but it promises to redefine the very notion of music for creators and listeners alike, igniting a creative renaissance in the world of sound.

And so, the symphony of innovation continues, painting the horizon with melodies that echo the beats of a new era in music production and composition. Stage currently cleared, cue to start playing!

Chapter 4. Making Melodies in the Metaverse: An Introduction to VR Tools

Virtual reality (VR), the encompassing medium that maneuvers our sensory and perception practices, is virtually reshaping a new landscape in the realm of music composition and production. As we dive into this radical transformation, prepare to traverse unprecedented terrain, exploring novel methods of generating melodies.

4.1. The Birth of VR in Music Creation

Rewinding to the genesis of this symbiosis between VR and music, it's worth recognizing the underpinning propellant: innovation. Early pioneers, such as Ge Wang, who developed the Ocarina, and Björk, who launched a VR project that captured the essence of each track from her album Vulnicura, set the stage for today's cavalcade of immersive music experiences. Harnessing the VR interface to kinetically interact with and perceive music empowers us with an extraordinary creative canvas, leveraging the depth of the three-dimensional plane that VR inhabits.

Our understanding of interactions with musical tools is challenged and revolutionized, eliminating the necessity for tactile complexity and offering a thrillingly intuitive and immersive realm in which harmonic structures can thrive and evolve. The aim is towards a seamless integration between the human and the tool, resulting in a symbiotic relationship, the two components merging and interacting to build the auditory masterpiece.

4.2. Embracing VR: Tools and Software

Chartering the VR domain, numerous tools and software have emerged to shift the paradigm of melody production. Amid the myriad offerings, we'll focus on a few notable ones that balance innovation and accessibility.

The first we'll dive into is SoundStage, an intuitive music sandbox built specifically for room-scale VR. Whether you're a professional studio producer or a novice, SoundStage offers an array of virtual instruments – drums, synthesizers, samplers, sequencers – and even a platform to construct your own instruments.

Think of VR as a vast expanse, and SoundStage as your palette of auditory paints; you are free to blend the tones as you like, creating an endless variety of musical landscapes. The interface demands no prior technical expertise, erases conventional physical constraints, and places the user at the center of the creative process, then wrapping them in a 360-degree soundscape.

Another notable tool is LyraVR. Known as a "virtual symphony playground," LyraVR propels the user into a sonic world where you compose, perform, and share musical compositions. The platform extends its functionality, allowing to manipulate the position, dimension, and dynamics of each sound emitter, thus influencing the spatial characteristics of the melodies.

4.3. The 3D Composition Interface

The real revolution in using VR for music comes from the unique 3D interface it offers. Unlike traditional music production systems that are limited to a two-dimensional plane, VR fills the space around the composer. This offers unprecedented freedom to position, manipulate, and experiment with sound in a three-dimensional environment. In this unlimited space, users can physically place musical notes and generate rhythmic patterns in the area around them, forging intricate connections between the aural and visual.

Imagine dangling notes in the air, flinging beats around in a rhythmic pattern, or dragging bass lines across the room. The VR interface reinforces the visualization of melodic and harmonic structures, facilitating manipulation of musical elements by merely reaching out and touching them.

4.4. The Spatial Audio Advantage

VR also introduces another crucial feature known as spatial audio or 3D sound. With the help of HRTF (Head-Related Transfer Function) technology, sounds can be manipulated to appear as if they originate from any point in the three-dimensional space, thereby creating a compellingly immersive auditory experience. This technology simulcasts the acoustics of reality by considering the minute details related to human anatomy and its interaction with sound waves.

Spatial audio is not merely an audio enhancement; it's a narrative tool that augments the storytelling capabilities of VR compositions. Harmonic arrangements can now sculpt an auditory landscape, guiding the listener's attention, bolstering emotional responses, and crafting a nuanced soundscape that matches the visual sophistication of VR.

4.5. Bridging Virtuosity and Virtual Reality

Melding VR with music composition weaves an engaging narrative for virtuosos and enthusiasts alike. It's not merely about creating tunes; it's about inducing an immersive adventure within a musical construct.

Through VR, creators can, for the first time, step inside their compositions, interacting and tweaking the music from within this personal soundscape. Conversely, audiences gain previously unthinkable access, able to inhabit the musical realm the artist has crafted, experiencing the narrative flow of the composition from every sonic angle.

Embarking on the journey of creating tunes using VR tools is admittedly a thrilling exploration that reconceptualizes the traditional form of music composition. The blend of VR tools and music can tantalize the senses, giving birth to a refreshing palette of melodic symphonies that echo the rhythm of the future.

4.6. Final Note

VR is indeed a burgeoning revolution, an immersive technology that oscillates the cursor of music making towards more intimate creator-medium intimacy. Charged with such potent tools, it's an exciting era for composers, producers, and music-lovers to harmonize their interaction with melodies, creating a much more personal yet revolutionary musical departure from the traditional norm. In the sphere of music, VR is the new maestro, orchestrating a symphony that resonates with the rhythm of innovation.

Chapter 5. Immersive Compositions: Understanding VR Soundscapes

In recent years, the advance of virtual reality (VR) technology has unlocked a new dimension in musical expression - the creation of immersive soundscapes. These sonic universes are designed to envelop the listener, delivering a powerful, three-dimensional audio experience that pushes the boundaries of traditional music production. VR's potential to revolutionize sound and music isn't contingent upon the future; it's unfolding right now. Let's delve into this exciting world and unearth its implications for the field of music.

5.1. The Essence of Immersive Sound

Essentially, music in virtual reality, or immersive sound, pertains to full-spatial audio that changes as the user navigates their virtual environment. In VR, there are no traditional left and right channels. Sounds come from every direction - above, below, in front, behind, and all around. Distinct from stereo or surround sound, the immersive audio in VR mimics how we hear sounds in the real world.

An important component of this design is sound localization. In a VR environment, each sound has a precise location in three-dimensional space. This means that as a user moves around, the direction, volume, frequency, and even the speed of sound must change accurately according to their virtual position and motion, creating a more realistic and compelling VR experience.

However, transforming static, two-dimensional soundscapes into dynamic, three-dimensional ones isn't a straightforward task. It necessitates an intricate blend of technology, psychoacoustics - the human perception of sound - and artistry.

5.2. VR Tools for Creating Immersive Soundscapes

Catering to this rapidly developing field, a growing number of software tools and systems are becoming available to composers working with VR. Software such as Tilt Brush by Google and VRScout allow for visual artistry in VR, and the musical equivalent tools are beginning to emerge.

For instance, Google's Resonance Audio and Facebook's Spatial Workstation are two such pioneering tools used by musicians to build immersive soundscapes. These applications provide innovative ways to manipulate sounds in a full 3D environment. They enable VR composers to mimic real-life sounds or create hyperreal soundscapes that stretch reality.

In addition, there exists a novel category of instruments - namely, VR instruments - which make creating music inside VR environments possible. LyraVR and EXA: The Infinite Instrument are two primary examples. These instruments allow composers to manipulate sounds in a spatial 3D environment, creating a unique musical space.

5.3. Crafting Melodies in Virtual Reality

The process of creating music for VR is significantly different from traditional methods, largely due to the three-dimensional component of immersive sound. This aspect necessitates a new approach in the composition phase where the spatial placement and movement of sounds is considered.

Instead of solely focusing on the harmony, melody, and rhythm, composers must consider how sounds move and exist within the 3D sound field. They need to visualize how an instrument's sound might come from behind or above, how the intensity of a sound might change as a listener moves closer, or how ambient background noise will interact with the principal musical elements.

This crafting process is both a technical and creative challenge. On the technical front, composers must master new software and instruments. Simultaneously, from a creative standpoint, they must envisage music not just in time but also in space - a concept they have not previously dealt with.

5.4. Breaking the Fourth Wall of Music

One of the substantial changes VR offers is 'participatory' music experiences. Normally, music is a passive listening experience. However, immersive soundscapes break the fourth wall much like in theater, allowing people to explore, interact with, and even alter the sounds around them.

Music in virtual reality can thus be adaptive or reactive to the listeners' actions, providing an enhanced, deeply personal engagement with the music. This level of interaction can create unique and profound experiences and mark a significant shift in the listener's role – as they transition from mere audience members to active participants in the music.

What's more, in VR, music and sound can serve a more integrated role in storytelling and create a sense of 'presence' – a feeling of being 'inside' the music or story, thereby amplifying emotional responses.

5.5. The Evolution of Listening Experience

The shift from conventional listening to immersive soundscapes is a significant one. Traditional stereo or even surround sound doesn't allow for personal exploration of the soundscape, nor does it offer the level of spatial comprehension that VR does.

In immersive VR soundscapes, rather than sitting passively and receiving the music from a fixed set of speakers, listeners can explore the music environment fully. They can choose to move closer to a particular sound, such as a solo instrument or singer, experiencing the parts of the composition in new ways.

As we venture deeper into the VR soundscape, we're starting to understand that VR isn't just a different platform for music. It's a whole new canvas that provides a paradigm shift in how we create, present, and interact with sound.

Virtual Reality is just beginning to influence the realm of music production and composition. As it reshapes our understanding of sound and breaks new ground in our experience of music, we are standing on the precipice of an exhilarating revolution. Today's exploration and innovation in the virtual sphere promise to ripple into the future, bringing with it a symphony of unimagined possibilities.

Chapter 6. Resonating Frequencies: Technical Aspects of VR Music Production

The aesthetics of music creation have long been intertwined with technology. As we dive into the specifics of VR in music production, it's important to understand that three main components are at the center: the VR hardware, the software applications, and the sounds (or instruments) used to create music.

6.1. VR Hardware for Music Production

The first point of contact between a music producer and VR is the hardware. Contemporary VR systems, including headsets such as the Oculus Rift, HTC Vive, and PlayStation VR, offer an immersive visual and aural experience.

However, creating music within VR extends beyond a captivating visual interface. High-quality headphones are crucial for music and sound production, as well as spatial audio, a critical facet of VR that replicates how humans perceive sound in different environments.

Moreover, specialized controllers like the Oculus Touch or the Vive Tracker provide a nuanced, tactile interface, allowing producers to interact with virtual tools, akin to picking up an instrument and playing.

6.2. VR Software for Music Production

Several applications have emerged that take advantage of VR hardware capabilities, creating novel ways to interact with music. These range from music creation software, allowing users to compose, mix, and master tracks within VR, to live performance tools that let you DJ, play instruments, or conduct visual effects.

SoundStage VR, for instance, provides a toolkit akin to a 'fantasy studio', allowing producers to synthesize sounds, build drum machines, or physically scope out a mixer on a virtual board. Another example, Lyra VR, lets you piece together elements of a composition in a physically realistic manner, creating notes and melodies that float in the space around you.

6.3. Sonics: Sounds and Instruments in VR

A crucial realization is that virtual reality extends beyond the visual. VR in music production allows us to literally sculpt sound. The traditional idea of a synthesizer or a drum pad can be tossed aside when you start crafting sounds in the three-dimensional space around you.

Software applications offer an array of virtual instruments which provide the same, if not better, kind of control as their physical counterparts, augmented with some added VR bonuses. For example, an immersive piano virtual instrument can have virtually limitless keys, straying away from the physical limitations of a traditional piano.

VR music also encourages the rethinking of instruments altogether. Even a deeply familiar instrument, like a guitar, can become an immersive environment where each string is a melody or rhythmic generator.

6.4. Spatializing Sound and Music

One of the most exciting parts of VR music production is the concept of spatializing sound. In a VR environment, sound isn't just stereo; it occupies the three-dimensional space around the listener. Applications such as AudioShield utilize this spatial characteristic for musical gameplay, transforming tracks into physical entities to interact with.

In a music production context, spatialization allows for new methods of composition and arrangement. Sounds can literally 'encircle' the listener, move around them, or appear from different distances. This dynamic element of spatial audio is a powerful tool for composers and offers an untouched frontier for sonic design.

6.5. Perspectives on Performance and Creation

What's truly revolutionary about VR music production is a shift of perspective. It turns music production from a task-focused activity based on small, intricate adjustments on computer interfaces to a fully immersive, performative act.

New solutions like AliveIn's tech, which turns dance movements into music, blur the lines between performer and producer. DJing tools like Vinyl Reality allow you to engage with a performance in a realistic manner, but with features and possibilities that far surpass even the most advanced physical DJ decks.

Similarly, conductive gloves like the ones developed by Imogen Heap's MI.MU project translate movement into sound, adding a performative, almost choreographic aspect to music creation.

The maturation of VR technology provides a unique opportunity to revisit the foundations of music production. The convergence of sound and vision within an immersive three-dimensional space opens new avenues for creative expression and audience experience. While we are still at the beginning of this journey, the harmony between VR and music is brewing an audacious symphony of innovation, encapsulating technology, artistry, and sound.

Chapter 7. Breakthroughs in Beat-making: Drumming in the Virtual World

Imagining a world where physical instruments are replaced by virtual iterations seems like a sci-fi narrative. But hold on before you dismiss it. The realm of Virtual Reality (VR) is expanding, reaching into the previously untrodden domain of music production, sneaking into the drummer's studio, and offering an enthralling alternative: Virtual Drumming.

7.1. Unleashing Creativity in a Virtual Studio

By transforming the traditional equipment-laden studio into an expansive, interactive VR environment, artists are handed an infinite canvas for their creative exploration. In this digital realm, the constrictions of physical space dissipate. Imagine, instead of a standard drum kit, finding yourself amidst an array of holographic drums, each customizable to your desire. The ability to resize, relocate, and infinitely clone drums lends a novel spontaneity to beat-making. Throw your drum stick to the western digital sky and you might end up triggering a bass drum, while a higher stratospheric hit calls forth a snare drum.

This liberated milieu, wherein you regulate the rules, is the playground for unconventional musical compositions. The potential roaming space for sonic exploration becomes immeasurable when the virtual world enables musicians to venture outside their traditional understanding of an instrument.

7.2. The Rise of Intuitive Interactions

Key to this execution, however, is the development and implementation of intuitive interaction models. Remember, virtual drumming shouldn't mandate gamers' proficiency or a diploma in advanced technology. Uncomplicated and intuitive interactions form the heart of compelling VR experiences.

Leveraging haptic technology and real-time tracking, VR can mimic the physical feedback of striking a drum's surface. You feel the vibrations radiating through your virtual drum stick, hear the resonating sound in your headphones, and see the corresponding visual cue – a complete sensory immersion. Simplifying these interactions can help catalyze the adoption of VR in music production, making it particularly attractive to amateurs who might be overwhelmed by traditional drum sets.

7.3. Fine-Tuning the Details

Nothing beats the tangible thrill of drumming: the subtle rebound after a stick hits, the different tones achieved by varying pressure, or the instant vibration feedback. Capturing these nuanced attributes in the virtual realm is the key challenge. Here, developers turn to haptic feedback technologies that aim to recreate these subtleties in the virtual space. Advanced tracking technology helps anticipate the user's movement and provides corresponding sensory feedback, resulting in an impressively realistic personal drumming concert.

7.4. Power of Visualization

A salient advantage to VR is its inherent capacity for visualization. In a virtual drum kit, color-coding different elements according to their sound type (e.g., yellow for cymbals, blue for snares), dynamically displaying rhythm patterns, or presenting real-time sound waveforms can greatly aid in understanding and producing complex beats.

7.5. Virtual Rehearsals and Performance

Bringing it full circle, VR can equip musicians with a virtual band. Interactive virtual musicians are no longer futuristic wishful thinking. Artists can rehearse with virtual band members, fine-tuning their timings and tweaking their parts, all within their very own VR studio. Sharing a virtually realistic space with digital companions creates an intimate band rehearsal experience, brushing aside logistical difficulties of gathering a band in one physical space.

7.6. Social Implications and Learning Benefits

When dove into the educational context, VR has the potential to democratize drumming. Drum sets are bulky, expensive, and loud – factors that often hinder accessibility. But VR can break down these barriers, making drumming cheaper, quieter, and more compact.

As a social tool, VR also allows for distant collaborations. Imagine jamming in real time with a drummer across the globe or joining a virtual drum circle. Besides, teachers and students can exist in the same virtual space, making distance learning a tangible reality.

Pounding the air might not immediately replace the deep-rooted tradition of pounding drums. But the story of drumming in a virtual world is yet unfolding, awaiting novelties and advancements with each beat. It is re-imagining and re-engineering not just how drumming is experienced but also how music can be created, taught, shared and enjoyed. As technology fine-tunes its rhythm, this virtual paradigm forces us to reconsider our physical assumptions, inviting us into an unprecedented symphony of innovation.

Chapter 8. Case Studies: VR Success Stories in Contemporary Music

In recent years, Virtual Reality (VR) has set foot on the fertile dancefloors of the music industry, the intersection of VR with music production and composition is evolving into a beautiful symphony of innovation. Success stories are abundant, illustrating the transformative power VR holds in reshaping the landscape of contemporary music production. In the following sections, we will delve deeper into a variety of case studies, providing an in-depth view on how VR is altering the way music is produced, composed, and ultimately experienced.

8.1. Bjork's 'Vulnicura' VR Album Experience

Pioneering the creative use of VR in music, Icelandic singer-songwriter Bjork debuted her 'Vulnicura' VR album in 2015. This ground-breaking project was a trailblazer in the music industry, manifesting as an immersive VR experience that accompanied her emotional journey through heartbreak. Each song from the album was created as an individual VR experience. Users found themselves in digitally-rendered worlds, where they explored unique landscapes for each track. Bjork's VR album signifies a perfect blend of cutting-edge technology and emotional storytelling, ultimately crafting an immersive, multi-sensory experience that propels music into another dimension. This case marks a landmark in VR integrated music production, setting a benchmark for other artists to explore and innovate.

8.2. TheWaveVR: Redefining DJ Performance

TheWaveVR is a trailblazing social VR platform that's revolutionizing how DJs perform and interact with their audiences. Users can attend live shows, customized by the performing DJs, creating a shared venue for music lovers to interact, dance, and feel the beat in a uniquely immersive environment. Beyond the shared experience, this platform pushes the boundary of interactive music experiences by empowering users to remix tracks and create their own beats in VR. TheWaveVR demonstrates the potential of VR not only in music consumption but also music creation, inspiring a new generation of DJs to embrace the digital realm.

8.3. Sigur Ros and Magic Leap Collaboration: Tónandi

In a groundbreaking collaboration, post-rock band Sigur Ros and tech company Magic Leap pushed the limits of sensory experiences by developing a generative soundscape app, "Tónandi". As users explore the app's otherworldly environment, the music responds interactively to their movements, resulting in a deeply personal and dynamic composition unique to each user. Tónandi offers a compelling glimpse into how VR technology can foster an intimate interaction between artists and their fans by creating an interactive and personal music experience.

8.4. VR Music Videos: Gorillaz's 'Saturnz Barz'

The Gorillaz, a British virtual band, rode the wave of VR and released the music video for 'Saturnz Barz' in 360-degree VR format. The narrative-driven video offered fans a new perspective to the music, guiding them through the intricacies of sonic and visual storytelling. Fans were able to experience an animated universe designed by the band, enveloping them in an immersive experience. The success of 'Saturnz Barz' marked another milestone for VR in music, demonstrating its potential to evolve traditional music video formats into sophisticated, multi-dimensional narratives.

8.5. Grimes and Endel Collaboration: AI Lullaby

Though less traditional, the marriage of music and VR shouldn't overshadow the promising union of augmented reality (AR) and music. This was proven when artist Grimes partnered with Endel to create AI Lullaby, an AR soundscape intended to foster better sleep and relaxation. By combining machine learning and Grimes' ethereal soundscapes, the app curates personalized sound journeys designed to help users unwind. This AR and music partnership points toward the future of personalized and dynamic music experiences.

8.6. RAM by Daft Punk: The VR Experience

In 2013, Daft Punk released the album 'Random Access Memories (RAM)', but alongside it, a VR experience was developed that enhanced the musical journey of their fans. The VR experience involved different unique virtual environments for each track, extending the relationship between the listeners and the album. The VR journey provided a new platform for listeners to experience and interact with their music, fortifying the path of VR in music composition and production.

8.7. Conclusion

These explorations and experiments all contribute to the expanding panorama of VR adoption in the music arena. The case studies explored above unearth the potential of VR to transform conventional music experiences into intricate, personalized arenas of multi-sensory engagement. As artists push boundaries and technologies mature, the fusion of VR and music is opening new dimensions of creativity, innovation, and interaction. Given the promising trend, it's clear the symphony of VR and music production has only just begun. The industry eagerly awaits the dawn of new technological advancements propelling this trend forward, making the music listening experience a journey, and the process of music creation, a novel pleasurable escapade.

Chapter 9. Crescendo in the Creative Process: Enhancing Composition with VR

In the expanding universe of music, the process of creation, a reverberating exchange of ideas, emotions, and expressions, has been revolutionized through the profound influence of Virtual Reality (VR). An innovative and transformative technology, VR represents an instrumental breakthrough in the composition process, functioning as an open-source orchestra that invites composers to curate their unique virtuoso from a harmonic ensemble of limitless possibilities.

9.1. The Symphony of Innovation: VR Meets Music

In an exhilarating symphony of innovation, VR has rapidly immersed itself into the field of music composition. It has boldly broken the constraints imposed by traditional music composition tools and software, replacing them with an interactive, immersive, and intuitive experience. VR offers composers an unprecedented level of control and creative freedom, integrating physical movement, spatial awareness, and three-dimensional design into the very fabric of musical composition.

Imagine sweeping your arm through the air, shaping the rhythm, and adjusting the tone of your composition as naturally as breathing. Embracing VR, you can interact directly with your music, translate your imaginative designs into audible reality, manipulating the altitude, pitch, intensity, and much more with compelling certainty.

9.2. The Maestro's New Tool kit: VR Instruments and Software

The true power of VR lies not only in the way it enhances the experience of music creation but also in how it revolutionizes the tools for composition. Innovative VR software and applications have begun to reshape the defining boundaries of musical instruments, offering composers an unbounded palate of sounds and a resonant orchestra of virtual instruments at their fingertips.

These tools play a significant role in creating a flexible environment that is conducive to varied creative workflows. VR instruments, like AliveIn VR, LyraVR, and Soundstage, offer an array of uniquely designed musical instruments and interfaces, ranging from MIDI controllers and electronic keyboards to dynamic drum kits and harmonious harps.

Effectively, the complexity and logistics of sound design, something previously virtually impenetrable by those not specifically schooled in it, has now become far more accessible and democratic, allowing anyone to create and shape sounds in their own way.

9.3. Free-form Composition: Interactive Music Creation

Historically, composition has been a complex, multifaceted process involving detailed knowledge of musical principles, notation, and intricate software applications. With the advent of VR tools, however, the composition process has transformed into free-form, interactive, collaboration.

Music creation in VR is incredibly tactile and intuitive. Music-makers can shape their arrangements physically, manipulating virtual instruments directly through movements that translate seamlessly into musical inputs. Finger placement and gesture translate to notes and chords, and the pace of your movements can directly control the speed, rhythm, and tone of the music. This translucent layer of interactivity not only makes composition more expressive but also more accessible to newcomers, who can now experiment, learn, and adapt in a more hands-on approach.

9.4. Song Sketching: Visualizing Music Through VR Space

An exceptional advantage of VR is its ability to interpret and manipulate spatial relations that transcends the tangible, physical environment. In the virtual realm, the spatial arrangement of instruments, the proximity of the sound sources, and the acoustic design of the virtual environment can be astutely adjusted and personalized.

Song sketches, for instance, allow composers to visualize their music, adding a dynamic dimension to composition. These sketches can create audio maps, which provide a spatial representation of how the composition unfolds in time and space. This visualization aids composers in understanding the structure and progression of their music, making the creative process more explicit and lucid.

Through VR, the composition process no longer consists of an abstract, solitary experience confined to a traditional linear timeline, but rather an immersive journey through melody and rhythm, that is every bit as creative as it is innovative.

9.5. The Future Harmony of VR and Music

The rhythm of music evolution grows ever more enchanting with each passing moment due to the symphonic integration of VR. With the promise of transforming the way we perceive, interpret, create, and engage with music, VR is reshaping the musical landscape into an audacious soundscape of limitless potential and boundless creativity.

The technology is yet in its infancy, and VR's contribution towards democratizing the world of music is just the beginning of an overwhelmingly melodious discourse in the realm of composition and production. As more musicians adopt and adapt to this new tool, and as technology itself continues to evolve and progress, the true potential of VR in music production is yet to be fully realized.

So, immerse yourself in this harmonious future. Embrace the rhythm of creativity. Dive into the symphony of innovation. Because your next composition could be writing the history of the new era in music. Through VR.

Chapter 10. The Sound of the Future: Predicting Music Trends with VR

In the realm of music production, one can never predict precisely how innovations will morph the way we hear, feel, and create music. But as technology shifts gears and plunge head-first into a future powered by Virtual Reality (VR), we can argue convincingly that we stand on the precipice of a seismic transformation - an avant-garde era when music and VR intersect to create auditory experiences that reverberate far beyond sound.

10.1. VR: The New Maestro

Enter VR - the buzzword of the tech industry, which is steadily permeating into the echelons of music production. VR is weaving a virtual web, encapsulating not only gamers and tech enthusiasts, but also musicians, producers, and their audiences. The question is no longer about what VR is, but rather, how it is transforming the act of composing music and predicting future trends.

The power of VR lies in its immersive nature; it has the capacity to transport you to hyperrealistic alternate realities or surreal, abstract landscapes, making a perfect canvas for the musical arts. Think of it as the new maestro, dictating the direction, pitch, rhythm, and tempo, but with a twist. As opposed to merely envisioning the composition, artists entrench themselves in it, morphing the musical panorama by tweaking the pitch here and modifying the rhythm there.

10.2. Engaging Audiences with Immersive Music Experiences

The flip side of the coin is the audience, and VR offers a promising way of engaging the listener, morphing passive listeners into active participants. Audiences can interact with the musical piece, tailor their listening settings, and even alter the composition, directly impacting the creation and consumption of music.

The trend points towards a more engaged listener base, with interactive concerts and performances. Artists such as Billie Eilish and Travis Scott have already been taking advantage of this trend, offering VR concerts where fans can immerse themselves in the experience from their homes. The success of such undertakings yet again underscores the potential of VR in reshaping the music industry.

10.3. New Dimensions in Music Training

But how does VR factor into the formative phase i.e., music education? VR is turning the traditional teaching methods on their heads by allowing aspiring musicians to practice in a VR environment. This hands-on approach provides instant feedback, therefore, adding a new dimension altogether to music training.

Learning music through VR could potentially be the norm in the not-so-distant future. Educational institutions are already investigating these possibilities, helping students better understand music theory, harmonic progression, and the association between different sounds.

10.4. Sound Sculpting and Spatial Audio

VR also lends a three-dimensional edge to music while making spatial audio and sound sculpting a hot trend. This involves the listeners' immersion in a 360-degree sound landscape, enabling them to experience the music's physicality.

With sound sculptures, artists can place different sounds in various areas of the VR environment, letting listeners walk through the music piece, modifying the sound as they move. This presents a whole new perspective on music composition, potentially ushering in a fresh age of spatial compositions.

10.5. Predicting the Unpredictable

In this rapidly changing scenario, predicting a singular future for music through VR may seem like a futile endeavor. However, based on current trends, it's safe to predict a more interactive future for the music landscape.

Artists and listeners will likely engage through immersive music experiences, concerts, and trainings. Spatial audio and sound sculpting will become integral parts of the creative process. Coupling all these with AI and machine learning technologies can enable artists to create complex and sophisticated compositions with lesser effort and time - eventually democratizing the music creation space.

10.6. The Future Resounds

While it's essential to keep grounded in the here and now, we must also celebrate the doors that VR can open for the music industry. After all, it's not just about the sound of music. It's about experiencing it, feeling it, and being completely immersed in it –

something that VR promises to deliver.

Remember, though, that technology can only enable creativity, not replace it. So even as VR is set to change the future of music, the human element remains central. At its core, music is about resonating with human emotions, connecting hearts, and inspiring souls. As we embark on this exciting new journey, VR should serve as a tool that furthers this vision.

In conclusion, it's essential to remember that music, at its core, will always belong to the creators - the composers, musicians, singers, and producers who breathe life into melodies. Virtual reality, with its immersive potential, provides a new wave of creative opportunities. But at the end of the day, it is the human touch that truly makes the music come alive. If nothing else, that is something that will never change, regardless of technology's overwhelming grip.

The future of music, it seems, is not only to be heard but to be seen, felt, and experienced. Only time will tell how we tune into this tantalizing symphony of possibilities. But until then, let's keep our ears, minds, and souls open to the profound rhythms of this promising new world.

Chapter 11. Concluding Cadence: The Enduring Impact of VR in Music

The advent of virtual reality (VR) in music presents a transformative era for music production and composition. With a host of strategic implementations, the VR platform is creating an immersive experience for artists and audiences alike, augmenting the interaction with music, and in the process, changing the face of the music industry.

11.1. Advancements in VR technology and their Impact

The advancement in VR technology has introduced tools like Google's Tilt Brush, which allows users to paint in a three-dimensional space, and Wave-VR which has already been used by artists to host virtual reality concerts. With such dynamic alterations in the tools available to musicians, there is an unprecedented opportunity for expression and engagement with music in reality and virtual space alike.

VR's contribution to the music scene isn't just novelty, though; it's opening up extensive possibilities for creative output. A traditional music setup may tend to confine musicians to physical boundaries, limiting them to playing one instrument at a time. However, VR can grant musicians the power to manipulate music from a whole different dimension, allowing them to navigate through soundscapes and even 'touch' music. The spatial orientation of sound plays a critical role in creating an immersive audio environment, a complex endeavor that VR can simplify.

11.2. VR and Music Education

Advancements in VR technology are also facilitating improvements in music education, addressing some of the fundamental barriers that can make learning music challenging such as physical presence and accessibility to instruments. Tools like MelodyVR bring the music classroom to the student, allowing them to play with a variety of instruments virtually without needing access to them physically. This ease of accessibility could help democratize music education, opening up opportunities for eager learners no matter their location or financial capability.

Furthermore, VR can be a powerful tool for deeper learning, providing interactive environments that surpass traditional teaching methods. Students are no longer restricted to studying sheet music; with VR, they can interact with the musical notes and patterns, understand their relationships, and comprehend complex musical concepts more intuitively.

11.3. Enhancing the Concert Experience

Beyond production and education, VR has potential in live music experiences too. Amid the COVID-19 pandemic, live music took a significant hit, with concerts and festivals worldwide canceled or postponed. However, artists quickly turned to virtual platforms, and it was here that the potential of VR shone through. With VR, artists could transcend geographical barriers to meet their fans, performances could be infinitely more immersive and personalized, and fans could experience live music right from their living room but feel like they're on stage with their favorite musicians.

Artists are now experimenting with avatars, virtual stages, and interactive features to provide an enhanced concert experience. The

VR concert spaces are also potential grounds for collaborations, giving birth to spatial audio-visual art pieces that extend beyond music videos or live performances.

11.4. Future Predictions for VR in Music

The implementation of VR in the music industry is still in its nascent stages with vast untapped potential waiting to be explored. Future software advancements could enable even deeper interactivity, bringing more sophisticated tools for music production, composition, and live performances.

AI integrated with VR could also redefine music composition as we know it, suggesting chord progressions and melody lines or even composing entire songs in collaboration with human musicians. Artists will be able to create immersive musical narratives, and listeners will be able to experience music in a personalized way, based on their emotional responses and interactions.

Just as the advent of electricity gave birth to electronic music and transformed the music industry, the union of VR and music has the potential to create a new paradigm of musical creativity and consumption. It's clear that the impact of VR on music is not a passing phase but an enduring revolution that is set to persist and evolve deeper with time.

To conclude, VR in music is no mere footnote; it is a force to be reckoned with, set to transform how we create, learn, and experience music. Whether we are artists pushing the boundaries of creativity, students exploring music in a dimensional space, or listeners eager for more intimate and immersive live shows, the advent of VR ushers in a new era of exploration and opportunities in music. As we tune in to the symphony of the future, we witness the transformative potential of VR in music, and its enduring impact on the industry and the audiences alike.